Splish, Splash
A very first picture book

Nicola Tuxworth

LORENZ BOOKS

That car needs
a good cleaning...

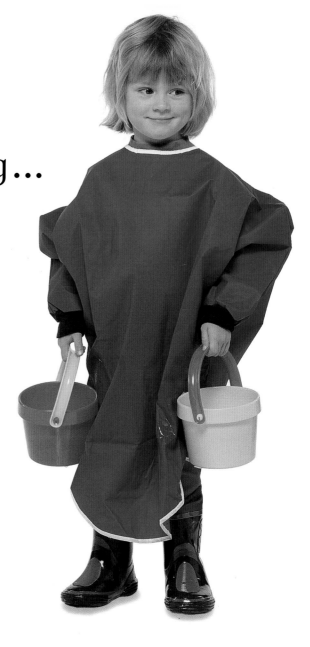

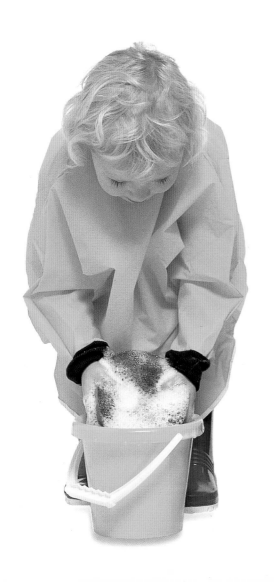

...with lots of
soapy water.

Splish,
splosh,
splash.

That looks
fun. Can
I help?

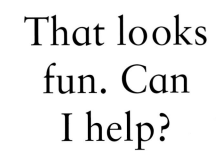

We're ready
to play in
the rain.

Wheee!
I'm jumping
in a puddle.

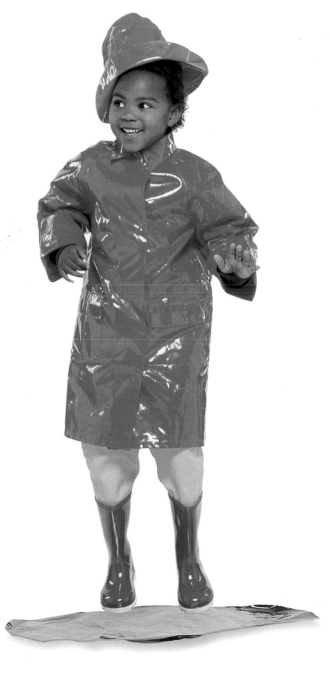

Whoops...

...I'm sitting
in a puddle!

I can wash myself.

Look at my new hairdo!

Where did
those three
ducks go?

Do you think we'll catch anything today?

Look!
We both
caught
whoppers!

Let's take
them home
for supper.

We're going to
water the flowers.

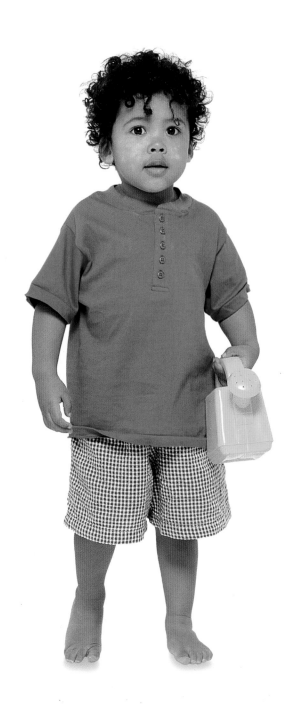

This sunflower needs
a lot of water.

My watering-can
is empty.

We like splishing
and splashing with
our hands.

We like sploshing with our feet.

Let's get
Mom
all wet!

Oh, no...

...I'm all wet!

We're going to feed the ducks.

Mmm ...
this tastes nice!

You look hungry!

We like splishing and splashing too!

Swish, swash with my trunk.

Paddle, paddle with my paws.

Whoosh, swoosh with my wings.

Gargle, gargle with my mouth.

Publisher: Joanna Lorenz
Managing Editor, Children's Books:
    Sue Grabham
Special Photography: John Freeman
Stylist: Thomasina Smith
Design and Typesetting:
    Michael Leaman Design Partnership

Thanks to: Mark Bloodworth, Freddy Cassford,
Alice Crawley, Lauren Ferguson, Safari George,
Saffron George, Jasmine Haynes, Joseph
Haynes, Erin Hoel, Charlotte Holden, Jack
Matthews, Megan Orr, Jimmy Pain, Philip
Quach, Eloise Shepherd and Nicola Tuxworth
for modeling for this book.

Picture credits: Papilio Photography: mute swan;
Zefa Picture Library Ltd: elephant, dog and
hippopotamus.

Printed in Hong Kong / China
10 9 8 7 6 5 4 3 2